JOSH STEVE

A Financial Crime Saga

Copyright © 2023 by Josh Steve

All rights reserved. No part of this publication may be reproduced, stored or transmitted in any form or by any means, electronic, mechanical, photocopying, recording, scanning, or otherwise without written permission from the publisher. It is illegal to copy this book, post it to a website, or distribute it by any other means without permission.

This novel is entirely a work of fiction. The names, characters and incidents portrayed in it are the work of the author's imagination. Any resemblance to actual persons, living or dead, events or localities is entirely coincidental.

Josh Steve asserts the moral right to be identified as the author of this work.

First edition

This book was professionally typeset on Reedsy. Find out more at reedsy.com

Contents

The Perfect Heist	1
The Insider	4
The Unraveling	8
The Double Cross	12
The Countdown	16
The Heist	19
The Chase	23
The Safehouse	27
The Puppetmaster's Lair	31
Shadows of Betrayal	35
The Shadow Broker's Game	39
The Consortium's Gambit	44

The Perfect Heist

The city's heartbeat pulsed through the darkened streets, its rhythm a chaotic symphony of sirens, car horns, and distant conversations. Rain lashed down from the ink-black sky, drenching the city in a shroud of secrecy. Amongst the shadows, a man named Daniel Mercer emerged, his footsteps echoing off the wet pavement as he hurried towards an inconspicuous building nestled between two towering skyscrapers.

The Raindrop Lounge, a place known only to those deep in the world of financial crime, was the venue for tonight's clandestine meeting. Its entrance, hidden behind a nondescript door, required a secret code whispered into a hidden intercom. Mercer, with a heart pounding in his chest, delivered the code: "Crimson Pinnacle."

The door slid open with a soft hiss, revealing a dimly lit, elegant lounge. The ambiance reeked of intrigue, with dark leather booths bathed in a soft, crimson glow. The clientele here were as discreet as the venue itself, their conversations hushed, their eyes sharp.

Mercer found a shadowy corner booth where a man in a tailored suit awaited him. His name was Victor Devereux, and he was the mastermind behind this audacious scheme.

"Daniel, right on time," Devereux purred, his fingers drumming lightly on a crystal glass filled with amber liquid.

Mercer nodded, his anxiety veiled by a calm exterior. He slid into the plush leather seat opposite Devereux, keenly aware of the gravity of this meeting. "You have the details?"

Devereux's steely gaze bore into Mercer's, assessing his resolve. Satisfied, he nodded and reached into his inner jacket pocket. He withdrew a manila envelope, thick with documents. "All the information you'll need to execute the perfect heist."

The envelope exchanged hands, and Mercer's fingers trembled ever so slightly as he felt the weight of its contents. The plan, meticulously outlined on crisp, cream-colored paper, included intricate diagrams, security protocols, and key access codes. It was a treasure trove of secrets, the blueprint for the greatest financial crime the city had ever seen.

"You have one month to prepare," Devereux cautioned. "The market is ripe, and the window of opportunity won't stay open for long."

Mercer's mind raced as he flipped through the documents. The heist would involve infiltrating a high-security financial institution, one that held a vault of black market bonds worth billions. These illicit securities were the lifeblood of the criminal underworld, coveted by all who dared to dream of unimaginable wealth.

The rain outside intensified, drumming against the lounge's windows like a persistent whisper of fate. Mercer couldn't help but wonder if this was the night that would change his life forever, or if it would all end in ruin.

"Remember, Mercer," Devereux whispered, leaning in closer, "this is a one-shot opportunity. The bonds must be extracted without a trace, and our involvement concealed. Failure is not an option."

Their eyes locked in a pact sealed by desperation and ambition. Mercer nodded, committing himself to the audacious plan that had been laid before him. He folded the documents back into the envelope, concealing the blueprint of their crime.

As he left the Raindrop Lounge, Mercer's heart was still racing, his steps now echoing with the weight of their conspiracy. The rain had transformed the city into a realm of secrets and uncertainty, a reflection of the dark path he had chosen. His mind swirled with questions, doubts, and the knowledge that the coming month would push him to the limits of his cunning and courage.

Outside, the world moved on, oblivious to the sinister design taking shape behind the scenes. In the heart of the city, hidden within the shadows, a financial crime saga was about to unfold—a saga driven by greed, desperation, and the relentless pursuit of the perfect heist.

The Insider

Three weeks had passed since Daniel Mercer's fateful meeting with Victor Devereux at the Raindrop Lounge. In that time, Mercer had immersed himself in the meticulously detailed plan for the perfect heist. Each day was a blur of stolen moments, covert research, and secret liaisons with the team he was assembling.

But tonight was different. Mercer had an appointment that would test his resolve like never before. He stood on a desolate street corner, under the flickering glow of a broken streetlight, anxiously checking his wristwatch. She was late.

Raindrops splattered on the cobblestone pavement, mimicking the rhythm of Mercer's racing heart. He had made contact with an insider, a woman named Evelyn Knox, who worked at the financial institution they intended to infiltrate. She was the key to their success—a mole on the inside.

Just as Mercer was beginning to doubt her commitment, he heard the soft click of high heels on the wet pavement. There she was, emerging from the shadows like a phantom. Evelyn Knox was a striking woman in her late thirties, with sharp green eyes that seemed to pierce Mercer's soul. Her trench coat billowed dramatically in the rain-soaked wind.

"You're late," Mercer said tersely, unable to hide his frustration.

Evelyn flashed a wry smile as she approached him, the raindrops glistening on her auburn hair. "Fashionably late, Mr. Mercer. It adds to the mystery, don't you think?"

Mercer clenched his jaw, trying to maintain his composure. He couldn't afford any loose ends in this operation. "Let's get to business," he said, gesturing for her to follow him into a nearby coffee shop.

Inside, the warmth of the café offered a stark contrast to the cold, unforgiving night outside. Mercer and Evelyn found a secluded corner booth, far from prying eyes and listening ears. Mercer placed a small recording device on the table, discreetly hidden beneath a sugar packet.

"Let's start with your role," Mercer began, his voice hushed. "You have access to the vault, correct?"

Evelyn nodded, her eyes locked on Mercer's with unwavering intensity. "I'm the assistant manager of the bank's security division. I oversee the vault's access codes, the surveillance systems, and the alarm protocols. I have the keys to the kingdom, Mr. Mercer."

Mercer's pulse quickened. The significance of her role could not be overstated. "Good. Our plan hinges on your cooperation. Can you disable the security systems on the day of the heist?"

Evelyn's smile was enigmatic. "I can disable the alarms, override the surveillance feeds, and even manipulate the time stamps to create a window of opportunity for you. You won't find a better insider."

Mercer couldn't help but feel a twinge of unease. Evelyn seemed almost too eager, too confident. He leaned in closer, lowering his voice to a whisper.

"What's in it for you, Ms. Knox? Why are you willing to betray your employer?"

Evelyn's gaze faltered for a moment, and Mercer sensed a vulnerability beneath her composed exterior. "Let's just say I have my reasons," she replied cryptically. "Reasons that go beyond money."

Mercer didn't press further. He knew better than to delve too deeply into her motivations. In this world of shadows and secrets, everyone had their own demons to contend with.

The rain continued to drum against the café's windows as they discussed the finer details of the plan. Mercer could hardly believe that this audacious scheme was on the verge of becoming a reality. The heist was scheduled for two weeks from tonight, and every day brought them closer to the point of no return.

As the meeting concluded, Mercer couldn't help but wonder if he could trust Evelyn Knox completely. The success of the heist hinged on her loyalty, and the consequences of betrayal were dire. He watched her disappear into the rainy night, her silhouette fading into the darkness.

Back in his apartment, Mercer reviewed his notes and the recording of the meeting. Doubt gnawed at the edges of his mind. Was Evelyn truly their salvation or a potential saboteur? The world of criminal conspiracies was fraught with peril, and Mercer knew that one misstep could lead to their downfall.

As the rain continued to pour outside, Mercer found himself wrestling with a sense of unease that refused to dissipate. The journey into the heart of darkness had only just begun, and the line between trust and treachery had never been thinner. In the days that followed, he would need to navigate this treacherous terrain with unwavering resolve, for the fate of the perfect heist hung in the balance.

The Unraveling

Two weeks remained until the date of the heist, and the tension in Daniel Mercer's life had reached a fever pitch. He had meticulously coordinated the team, fine-tuned the plan, and rehearsed every step of the operation. Yet, lurking beneath his facade of confidence, doubt gnawed at his insides like a persistent shadow.

The rain, relentless as ever, had become a constant companion, mirroring Mercer's mood. He paced the dimly lit room of his apartment, each step echoing like a countdown to destiny. He had just received a message on his encrypted phone—it was time for a meeting with Victor Devereux.

The Raindrop Lounge, shrouded in secrecy, was their designated meeting place once more. Mercer's heart raced as he navigated the rain-soaked streets. He knew that tonight's meeting was crucial; Devereux would want a progress report.

As Mercer entered the lounge, he scanned the dimly lit interior, searching for the familiar face of the man behind the audacious plan. He spotted Devereux in a corner booth, his eyes like steel under the crimson glow of the lounge's lighting.

"Daniel," Devereux greeted him with a nod, his voice as smooth as silk. "I trust everything is proceeding according to plan."

Mercer slid into the booth opposite Devereux, the weight of their mission settling heavily upon him. "We've assembled the team, and the preparations are nearly complete," he replied, carefully choosing his words. "But there have been... complications."

Devereux's brow furrowed, and his eyes bore into Mercer's with a mix of curiosity and impatience. "Complications? Explain."

Mercer hesitated for a moment, then decided to be forthcoming. "Our insider, Evelyn Knox, she's been acting strangely. She's confident in her ability to disable the security systems, but her motivations remain a mystery. I can't help but feel that she's hiding something."

Devereux leaned in, his gaze unwavering. "Are you suggesting she might betray us?"

Mercer paused, weighing his words carefully. "I don't know, but we can't afford to ignore the possibility. The success of this heist relies on her cooperation. If she falters, we're finished."

Devereux's fingers tapped rhythmically on the tabletop as he considered Mercer's words. "We'll need to keep a close eye on her. Ensure that she remains committed to the cause. This operation cannot afford any setbacks."

Mercer nodded, the gravity of their situation sinking in. This conversation had confirmed his own concerns, and he knew he had to take action. "I'll arrange a meeting with Evelyn," he said, "try to get to the bottom of her motivations."

Devereux regarded Mercer with a nod of approval. "Good. And remember, Mercer, we have come too far to let anything or anyone stand in our way.

The bonds in that vault are the key to our future."

The rain outside intensified, a symphony of despair echoing Mercer's inner turmoil. The path they had chosen was fraught with uncertainty, and he couldn't escape the feeling that they were dancing on the precipice of disaster.

Back in his apartment, Mercer couldn't shake the unease that had settled over him. He needed to confront Evelyn Knox, to unravel the mystery of her motivations. He arranged a secret meeting at a remote location, far from prying eyes.

Evelyn arrived, her eyes wary yet determined. Raindrops clung to her hair, making her appear like a figure from a noir film. Mercer wasted no time, plunging into the heart of the matter.

"Evelyn, we need to talk," he began, his voice low and intense. "Your commitment to this operation is paramount. I need to know that you're fully invested in our success."

Evelyn's gaze met his with a mixture of defiance and vulnerability. "You doubt me, Daniel?"

Mercer hesitated, torn between suspicion and the need for trust. "I need to understand your motivations, Evelyn. Why are you doing this? What's driving you to betray your employer?"

Evelyn's shoulders slumped, and for a moment, her mask of confidence crumbled. She looked away, her voice trembling as she spoke. "I have debts, Daniel. Debts that I can never repay. This operation is my only chance to escape the darkness that's closing in on me."

Mercer's heart ached for her, for the desperation that had led her down this treacherous path. He reached out and gently placed a hand on hers. "We're all in this together, Evelyn. We'll get through this, but I need to trust you completely."

She met his gaze, her eyes filled with a mixture of gratitude and determination. "You can trust me, Daniel. I won't let you down."

As the rain continued to pour outside, Mercer couldn't help but feel a glimmer of hope. The bond they had forged in that moment, amidst the rain and the secrets, might just be the key to their success. But the world of financial crime was a perilous one, and the challenges they faced were far from over.

The perfect heist was still on the horizon, a tantalizing promise of wealth and redemption. Yet, with each passing day, the shadows of doubt and uncertainty grew longer, threatening to engulf them all. In the end, it would be a test of their wits, their loyalty, and their determination to emerge from the darkness unscathed.

The Double Cross

The city had never felt more oppressive, its skyline looming like a fortress of secrets. As the days counted down to the planned heist, the weight of anticipation hung over Daniel Mercer like a relentless storm cloud. He had convened the team for a final briefing, a clandestine gathering in a dimly lit, underground speakeasy that bore no name.

Around a circular table, the members of Mercer's crew sat in the shadows, their faces obscured by the dim lighting. Among them were John "Slick" Reynolds, a safecracker with a reputation for getting into the most impenetrable vaults, and Maria "Silhouette" Sanchez, a master of disguise who could blend into any environment. But it was Evelyn Knox who commanded the room's attention, seated opposite Mercer.

The conversation had turned to the intricacies of the heist—the timing, the logistics, and the potential pitfalls. Mercer had been careful not to reveal his doubts about Evelyn, but he couldn't shake the feeling that something was amiss.

"As we all know," Mercer began, his voice a low, measured tone, "our success hinges on precise timing and coordination. Each of you has a critical role to play, and there's no room for error."

Slick leaned forward, his sharp eyes fixed on Mercer. "We've pulled off some tricky jobs, Mercer, but this one, it's something else. Are you sure we can trust our insider?"

All eyes turned to Evelyn, who met their scrutiny with unwavering resolve. "You can trust me," she said, her voice steady. "I've taken every precaution to ensure that our tracks are covered."

Maria, always perceptive, raised an eyebrow. "That's what concerns me," she said. "You're almost too confident. How can we be sure you won't betray us?"

Evelyn's jaw tightened, and Mercer sensed the tension in the room rising like a noose. "I have as much to lose as any of you," she replied, her voice tinged with frustration. "This operation is my way out, and I won't jeopardize it."

Mercer intervened, sensing that the conversation was taking a dangerous turn. "We're a team," he reminded them. "We've come too far to let distrust tear us apart. Our focus should be on the job ahead."

The tension lingered, but the meeting continued, shifting to the nitty-gritty details of the plan. Mercer outlined the timeline, the escape routes, and the contingencies for every possible scenario. With each passing minute, the heist took on a more ominous presence, like an unrelenting shadow waiting to engulf them.

As the meeting concluded, Mercer couldn't help but wonder if his concerns about Evelyn were unfounded. Perhaps she was simply a woman desperate to break free from her past. The crew dispersed into the night, each member burdened with the knowledge that their fate rested on the edge of a razor.

Mercer and Evelyn remained behind, a sense of unease hanging between them. "Evelyn," Mercer began, his voice a mere whisper in the dimly lit speakeasy, "I need to know that you're with us completely. No doubts, no secrets."

Evelyn's gaze met his, her green eyes holding a mixture of resolve and vulnerability. "I've risked everything for this, Daniel. You have my word."

But Mercer couldn't shake the feeling that something was amiss. He had built his life on instincts and intuition, and right now, those instincts were screaming at him. He had to dig deeper, to uncover the truth hidden beneath the layers of secrets.

Over the next few days, Mercer began discreetly probing into Evelyn's background. He traced her financial struggles, her debts, and the web of connections she had cultivated within the criminal underworld. The more he delved, the more he realized that her motivations were not as simple as they seemed.

One evening, Mercer received a message from an anonymous source—a cryptic note left in his mailbox. It read: "Watch Evelyn closely. She has secrets that could destroy us all."

The words sent a chill down Mercer's spine. Someone else had their eye on Evelyn, and they were warning him of a looming danger. He had to confront her, to unearth the truth before it was too late.

He arranged a meeting with Evelyn in a deserted parking garage, far from prying eyes. As he approached her car, he couldn't ignore the gnawing uncertainty that had taken root within him.

"Evelyn," he said as she stepped out of her car, "we need to talk."

Her eyes darted around nervously, and she seemed on edge. "What's this about, Daniel?"

Mercer didn't mince words. "I've received a warning about you. Someone thinks you're hiding something—something that could jeopardize the heist."

Evelyn's expression hardened, her guard rising. "And do you believe them?"

Mercer hesitated, torn between his growing suspicions and his desire to trust her. "I need to know the truth, Evelyn. Are you hiding something from us?"

Evelyn's silence was deafening, her eyes locked on Mercer's as if searching for answers within his gaze. Finally, she spoke, her voice trembling with uncertainty. "There are things in my past, Daniel, things I've kept hidden. But I promise you, they won't affect the heist."

Mercer studied her carefully, his instincts warring with his desire to believe her. "You need to tell me everything," he said, his voice firm. "We can't afford any surprises on the day of the heist."

Evelyn nodded, her shoulders slumping as if a heavy weight had been lifted. She began to speak, revealing a web of secrets and betrayals that ran deeper than Mercer could have imagined. Her past was a tapestry of deception, and the truth was more harrowing than he could have ever anticipated.

As the rain pelted the concrete floor of the parking garage, Mercer realized that their journey into the heart of darkness was far from over. The double-cross had been exposed, but the true extent of the betrayal remained uncertain. The heist was approaching, and the shadows of doubt and deception had cast a long, ominous pall over their carefully laid plans. In the world they inhabited, trust was a fragile commodity, and the line between allies and enemies blurred like a smudged ink stain on a page of secrets.

The Countdown

With just one week remaining until the planned heist, the air was thick with tension. Daniel Mercer had confronted Evelyn Knox about her secrets, and though she had revealed some unsettling truths from her past, there was a fragile sense of trust slowly rebuilding among the team. But the doubts still lingered, like shadows refusing to fade.

Each day, the crew worked tirelessly to finalize their preparations. In a rented warehouse on the outskirts of the city, they gathered to rehearse the heist one last time. Mercer had a countdown clock displayed on the wall, its digital numbers ticking away the hours, minutes, and seconds until the operation was set to commence.

Slick Reynolds stood before a replica of the vault's massive door, his gloved fingers poised to manipulate the intricate lock mechanisms. Mercer watched him closely, knowing that Slick's skill and precision were paramount to their success.

"Remember, Slick," Mercer cautioned, "timing is everything. We have a narrow window to get in and out of that vault."

Slick nodded, beads of sweat forming on his forehead as he concentrated on the mock vault. With practiced ease, he began to work, his nimble fingers dancing over the tumblers and dials.

Meanwhile, Maria Sanchez was perfecting her disguises, meticulously applying makeup and altering her appearance to match the bank's employees. She could transform into anyone, from a bank teller to a janitor, seamlessly blending into her surroundings.

As Mercer observed the preparations, his mind kept returning to Evelyn Knox. She had become an enigma, her past filled with shadows and betrayals. He wondered if there was more to her story, more secrets that could unravel their carefully laid plans.

Evelyn, aware of Mercer's scrutiny, approached him with a determined look in her eyes. "Daniel, I need to prove my commitment to this team," she said. "I know I've kept things from you, but I'm willing to do whatever it takes to make this heist a success."

Mercer regarded her for a moment, his thoughts swirling like a maelstrom of doubts and suspicions. "You'll have a chance to do just that," he replied cryptically.

As the day turned into night, Mercer gathered the team for a final briefing. They huddled around a table covered in blueprints, surveillance photos, and floor plans of the bank. The plan had to be flawless; there was no room for error.

"The heist is scheduled for 2:00 AM on Friday," Mercer began. "Evelyn will disable the alarms and surveillance systems. Slick, you'll take care of the vault door. Maria, you'll provide us with the perfect disguises."

The crew listened intently, their faces etched with determination. But Mercer couldn't ignore the lingering unease that hung in the air.

"Remember," he continued, "we only have a short window once we're inside the vault. We grab the bonds, exit, and disappear into the night. No heroics, no mistakes."

Slick, who had been practicing with the mock vault door, voiced a concern. "What if something goes wrong with the vault? What if we can't open it in time?"

Mercer had considered this possibility, and it weighed heavily on his mind. "If we can't open the vault, we abort the mission. It's not worth the risk of getting caught."

The crew nodded in agreement, but Evelyn's eyes were locked on Mercer, her gaze filled with a silent plea. Mercer knew she was desperate to prove herself, but the stakes were higher than any of them could imagine.

With the final briefing concluded, Mercer dismissed the team to get some rest. But he couldn't sleep. Instead, he found himself alone in his apartment, staring at the countdown clock on the wall. Each second that ticked away brought them closer to the moment of truth, and the weight of their impending actions bore down on him like an anvil.

In the darkness of the night, Mercer couldn't escape the gnawing doubts that clawed at the edges of his mind. The heist was on the horizon, a tantalizing promise of wealth and redemption, but it was also a perilous journey into the heart of darkness. The countdown had begun, and their fate hung in the balance, suspended between trust and betrayal, success and ruin.

The Heist

The night of the heist had arrived, shrouded in darkness and secrecy. A dense fog had rolled in from the river, obscuring the cityscape and muffling any sounds that might have carried through the night. It was the perfect cover for their audacious plan.

Daniel Mercer stood at the entrance of an inconspicuous building, his heart pounding like a drumbeat in his chest. The rain had stopped, but the air was heavy with tension. His team had gathered, each member disguised and equipped for the mission ahead.

Slick Reynolds adjusted the toolkit at his side, a confident glint in his eye. Maria Sanchez, transformed into the perfect bank employee, carried herself with an air of authority. And Evelyn Knox, her face hidden behind a mask of resolve, held the keys to their success—or their downfall.

"Remember the plan," Mercer whispered, his voice barely audible over the soft patter of raindrops. "We go in, grab the bonds, and get out. No mistakes, no deviations."

The team nodded, their expressions a mix of determination and apprehension. They had rehearsed the heist countless times, but the real thing was an entirely different beast.

Evelyn glanced at Mercer, her green eyes filled with a complex mix of emotions. "I won't let you down," she said, her voice filled with quiet conviction.

Mercer wanted to believe her, to put his doubts aside and trust in the unity of their team. But the shadows of uncertainty still loomed, and he knew that the night ahead would be their ultimate test.

They moved like ghosts through the city's winding streets, invisible to the casual observer. The bank, a formidable structure of steel and glass, stood as a sentinel in the night, its exterior illuminated only by the occasional flicker of security lights.

Evelyn led the way, her knowledge of the bank's security systems a precious asset. She navigated through a maze of alleys and service entrances, guiding the team to a discreet access point that had been meticulously planned.

Inside the bank, the air was stale, the hush of the late hour accentuated by the soft hum of fluorescent lights. The team members moved with purpose, their hearts racing in time with the ticking clock. There was no room for error.

Evelyn made her way to the security room, her fingers deftly bypassing the keypad. As she manipulated the controls, the surveillance cameras blinked out one by one, plunging the bank into darkness.

Maria, now clad in the uniform of a janitor, pushed a mop bucket filled with cleaning supplies down the corridor. She nodded to Mercer as she passed, her disguise affording her access to areas beyond the reach of typical employees.

Slick, dressed as a maintenance worker, was already at the vault door, his toolkit ready. He couldn't afford to make a mistake now; their entire plan depended on his expertise.

Mercer, wearing a suit and a fake ID badge, moved with the throng of bank employees heading to their respective offices. His heart pounded in his chest as he reached the elevator, his destination the upper floors of the building.

The vault was located in the heart of the bank, its imposing door a symbol of impenetrability. Slick worked with precision, the tumblers and dials yielding to his expertise. It was a delicate dance of skill and timing, and Mercer couldn't help but hold his breath as the final tumbler clicked into place.

The door to the vault swung open, revealing a cavernous chamber filled with rows upon rows of safety deposit boxes. And at the far end, the black market bonds, hidden within a secured vault within the vault, awaited them.

As Mercer stepped inside, the hairs on the back of his neck stood on end. The weight of the moment bore down on him like an avalanche of uncertainty. He glanced at Slick, who was already at work on the second door.

With bated breath, they entered the inner vault. The bonds, nestled within a secure compartment, were tantalizingly close. Mercer's heart raced as he reached for them, his gloved hands trembling with anticipation.

But just as he was about to grasp their prize, a blaring alarm shattered the silence. The vault's security systems had been reactivated.

Panic gripped Mercer as he heard the distant sound of approaching footsteps. They had run out of time.

Slick worked frantically to close the vault door, but it was too late. The intruder was nearly upon them.

Maria, her disguise abandoned, emerged from the shadows, a determined look in her eyes. "We have company," she whispered.

Evelyn, who had been guarding their escape route, joined them. "We need to move quickly," she urged. "The police will be here any minute."

Mercer knew that their options were dwindling, their fate hanging by a thread. They couldn't afford to be caught, not after coming this far.

With the bonds in hand, they retreated deeper into the vault, searching for an alternate exit. Their footsteps echoed in the cold, dimly lit chamber as they frantically scanned the surroundings.

Then, Mercer spotted it—a ventilation shaft large enough for them to crawl through. It was their only hope.

As the sound of approaching sirens grew louder, they crawled into the narrow confines of the shaft, leaving behind the tantalizing prize that had eluded their grasp. The bonds would have to wait; their escape was paramount.

In the cramped darkness of the ventilation shaft, Mercer couldn't help but wonder if they had been set up, if their daring heist had been nothing more than an elaborate trap. The answers remained elusive, and their journey into the heart of darkness had taken an unexpected turn.

As they crawled through the shadows, the distant wail of sirens served as a haunting reminder of the world they had entered—a world of secrets, betrayal, and a relentless pursuit of the perfect heist. In the darkness of the ventilation shaft, their fate remained uncertain, suspended between freedom and capture, trust and treachery, in a city where nothing was as it seemed.

The Chase

The air in the narrow ventilation shaft was stifling, suffocating, as if the walls themselves were closing in on Daniel Mercer and his team. Crawling through the darkness, their breath came in shallow gasps, their bodies pressed tightly against the cold metal surface. Behind them, the sound of approaching sirens grew louder, a relentless reminder of the peril they faced.

Mercer led the way, inching forward with grim determination. The plan had gone awry, their escape routes compromised, and the bonds they had risked everything for remained tantalizingly out of reach. He couldn't help but wonder if Evelyn Knox's past had caught up with them, if her secrets had led them into a carefully laid trap.

"We can't stay in here," Mercer whispered to the team, his voice echoing in the claustrophobic confines of the shaft. "We need to find a way out."

Slick Reynolds, crawling just behind Mercer, responded with urgency. "There's a maintenance exit ahead. It leads to the basement. It's our best chance."

Maria Sanchez and Evelyn Knox, their faces etched with determination, followed closely behind. Mercer couldn't deny the sense of unity that had formed within the team, forged through adversity and the relentless pursuit of their goal.

As they reached the maintenance exit, Mercer pushed the heavy door open, revealing a dimly lit basement filled with the humming of generators and the distant rumble of machinery. The sirens outside were now a cacophonous symphony of pursuit, drawing nearer by the second.

"We need to find a way out of here," Mercer urged, scanning the basement for an escape route.

Evelyn stepped forward, her voice determined. "There's an underground service tunnel that leads to a nearby sewer system. It's not ideal, but it might be our best bet."

With no other options, the team followed Evelyn as she led them deeper into the basement. The tunnel was narrow, with a low ceiling and a damp, earthy smell that clung to the air. Mercer couldn't help but think of the treacherous path they were now on, a descent into the very bowels of the city.

As they navigated the winding tunnel, the sounds of pursuit grew fainter, replaced by the distant echoes of their own footsteps. Mercer couldn't shake the feeling that they were being herded like rats into a trap, and he knew that their every move had to be calculated.

The tunnel seemed to stretch on endlessly, its darkness punctuated only by the feeble glow of their flashlights. Evelyn, leading the way, remained focused and determined, her motivations still a mystery to Mercer.

Finally, after what felt like an eternity, they emerged into a subterranean chamber filled with waist-high water. The stench was overpowering, a noxious mixture of sewage and decay. But it was their ticket to freedom.

"We'll need to wade through this," Evelyn said, her voice unflinching. "It leads to an exit near the river. From there, we can disappear into the night."

Without hesitation, the team began to wade through the putrid water, their steps slow and deliberate. The sounds of sirens were distant now, a mere whisper in the subterranean labyrinth. But Mercer couldn't shake the feeling that their troubles were far from over.

As they approached the exit, Mercer's flashlight beam caught something unsettling—a symbol painted on the damp, mossy wall. It was a crimson drop, the same symbol that had marked the entrance to the Raindrop Lounge, the place where their heist had been set into motion.

He couldn't help but wonder if this was more than mere coincidence. Had someone been watching them all along, orchestrating their every move?

Emerging from the tunnel, they found themselves on the banks of the river, the city's skyline looming in the distance. The night was eerily silent, the sirens now a distant memory. But Mercer knew that their escape had only just begun.

"We can't stay in the city," he said, his voice heavy with determination. "We need to disappear, lay low, and regroup."

Slick nodded, his face etched with exhaustion. "I know a safehouse in a nearby town. We can get there by dawn."

With a sense of purpose, the team set out along the river's edge, their steps taking them farther and farther from the city that had become a labyrinth of secrets and betrayal.

As they disappeared into the night, Mercer couldn't escape the haunting feeling that their ordeal was far from over. The pursuit, the doubts, and the relentless chase had left scars that ran deep. In this world of shadows and deception, trust was a fragile commodity, and their path forward remained uncertain. The chase had led them to the precipice, and the abyss of the unknown awaited, its depths concealed by the cloak of darkness.

The Safehouse

The night had deepened into an inky blackness as Daniel Mercer and his team continued their harrowing escape from the city. The rain had started to fall again, its cold, relentless droplets a cruel reminder of the perilous journey they were on. With each step, Mercer couldn't shake the sense that their every move was being watched, that they were mere pawns in a larger game of deception.

Slick Reynolds led the way, his flashlight cutting through the darkness as they followed a meandering path along the riverbank. The sound of rushing water was a constant companion, its soothing rhythm at odds with the tension that hung in the air.

"We're not far from the safehouse now," Slick announced, his voice low and measured. "Just a bit farther."

The team trudged onward, their fatigue hidden beneath a veneer of determination. Maria Sanchez, still dressed in her janitor's uniform, glanced back at Evelyn Knox, whose enigmatic presence seemed to weigh heavily on Mercer's mind.

"Are you okay?" Maria whispered to Evelyn, her voice tinged with concern.

Evelyn's response was a curt nod, her gaze fixed on the path ahead. Mercer couldn't help but wonder what was going on in her mind. Her secrets had already jeopardized their mission, and he couldn't afford any more surprises.

As they reached the outskirts of a small, rundown town, Slick led them to a nondescript building nestled among a row of dilapidated structures. It was their safehouse—a refuge from the chaos they had left behind in the city.

Inside, the safehouse was a dimly lit, sparsely furnished space. The air was heavy with the musty scent of disuse, and the room was filled with a sense of isolation. Mercer knew they couldn't stay here for long, but it was a temporary sanctuary.

"We'll rest here for a few hours," Slick said, his exhaustion evident in the weariness etched across his face. "We need to regroup and figure out our next move."

The team dispersed to different corners of the room, seeking solace in the brief respite. Mercer found himself alone with Evelyn, the unspoken tension between them palpable.

"Evelyn," he began, his voice a whisper, "we need to talk about what happened back there. The alarm, the police—was it a setup?"

Evelyn's gaze met his, and for the first time, he detected a hint of vulnerability in her eyes. "I don't know, Daniel," she admitted. "But I can't help but feel that someone knew we were coming. That symbol in the tunnel—it's the same one from the Raindrop Lounge."

Mercer's thoughts raced as he considered the implications. The symbol was a haunting reminder of their past, a connection to a web of secrets and betrayals. "We need to find out who's been pulling the strings," he said. "We can't afford to be pawns any longer."

Evelyn nodded, her determination resolute. "I'll do whatever it takes to uncover the truth, Daniel. But we need a plan."

As they spoke, Slick returned with a map spread out on the table. "I've been doing some digging," he said. "There's a contact I know, someone who operates in the underworld. He might have information on who set us up."

Mercer studied the map, tracing the route to the contact's location. "It's a risk, but we don't have much choice. We need answers."

With their plan in motion, the team had little time to rest. They knew that the pursuit wouldn't end until they had unraveled the mystery behind the heist and the symbols that had haunted their journey.

As they left the safehouse, the rain had intensified, shrouding the town in a gauzy mist. The contact's location was a dimly lit bar on the outskirts of town, its neon sign flickering in the downpour like a beacon of uncertainty.

Inside the bar, the air was thick with the acrid scent of cigarettes and the murmur of hushed conversations. Mercer's team gathered at a corner booth, their eyes scanning the room for any sign of their contact.

Moments later, a man in a worn leather jacket and a fedora approached their table, his face concealed in shadow. "You're the ones looking for answers," he said, his voice a gravelly whisper.

Mercer nodded, his voice equally low. "We need to know who set us up, who's been pulling the strings. We saw the symbol in the tunnel—what does it mean?"

The man regarded them with a sense of wariness. "You're treading in dangerous waters," he replied cryptically. "But I can give you a name—a name that might lead you to the truth."

He leaned in closer, his breath carrying the weight of secrets. "There's a man known as the Puppetmaster. He's a shadowy figure, a puppeteer who controls the criminal underbelly of this city. If anyone knows what's going on, it's him."

Mercer's heart

sank at the mention of the Puppetmaster. The name was infamous, a legend whispered in hushed tones among those in the know. To confront such a figure would be to court danger of the highest order.

"What do you want in return?" Mercer asked, his voice steady.

The man's eyes gleamed with a hint of avarice. "I need a favor," he said. "There's a rival I want you to eliminate. Do that, and I'll arrange a meeting with the Puppetmaster."

The team exchanged uneasy glances, but they knew they had little choice. They had ventured into a world of secrets and deception, and they couldn't turn back now.

With a nod of agreement, Mercer and his team left the bar, their path forward veiled in uncertainty. The Puppetmaster was a name that sent shivers down the spines of those who knew of him, and confronting such a figure would test their mettle like never before.

As they ventured deeper into the city's criminal underworld, the shadows of doubt and betrayal loomed large. The chase had led them to the precipice of a treacherous journey, one that would test their loyalty, their resolve, and their willingness to confront the darkness that lurked in the heart of the city. In this world of secrets and deception, the truth remained elusive, and their pursuit of answers was a relentless dance on the edge of danger.

The Puppetmaster's Lair

The night had taken on an ominous hue as Daniel Mercer and his team delved deeper into the criminal underbelly of the city, pursuing the enigmatic figure known as the Puppetmaster. The rain had transformed into a torrential downpour, drenching the streets and casting a shroud of darkness over their journey. Each step they took felt like a descent into the abyss of uncertainty.

Their contact had provided them with a location—a hidden lair on the outskirts of the city where the Puppetmaster was rumored to conduct his shadowy affairs. As they approached the address, Mercer couldn't help but feel a gnawing sense of unease. They were entering the domain of a figure whose power and influence were whispered about in hushed tones.

The building loomed before them, a decaying warehouse concealed in the cloak of night. Its windows were shattered, and the walls bore the scars of time and neglect. It was a place where secrets festered, and danger lurked in every shadow.

"We proceed with caution," Mercer warned the team, his voice low and steady. "We don't know what we'll find inside."

With flashlights in hand, they entered the dilapidated warehouse, the sound of rain echoing in the cavernous space. Mercer's senses were on high alert, every creak of the floorboards and rustle of debris setting his nerves on edge.

They ventured deeper into the darkness, their flashlights cutting through the obscurity like beams of hope in a desolate place. The air was thick with a sense of foreboding, as if the walls themselves held the memories of countless secrets.

As they explored the abandoned structure, they came across a series of interconnected rooms, each one shrouded in darkness. Mercer couldn't shake the feeling that they were being watched, that the Puppetmaster was aware of their intrusion.

Finally, they reached a room that seemed to hold a lingering presence. It was dimly lit by a single flickering bulb, casting long, distorted shadows on the peeling wallpaper. In the center of the room, an ornate wooden chair stood like a throne of obscurity.

And there, seated in the chair, was the Puppetmaster.

He was a figure draped in darkness, his features concealed by a wide-brimmed hat and a flowing trench coat. His hands, adorned with leather gloves, rested on the armrests of the chair. He exuded an air of malevolence that sent a shiver down Mercer's spine.

"You've come seeking answers," the Puppetmaster said, his voice a haunting whisper. "But answers come at a price."

Mercer stepped forward, his voice unwavering. "We want to know who set us up, who's been pulling the strings. The symbol—the Raindrop Lounge—what's the connection?"

The Puppetmaster leaned forward, his eyes hidden in the shadow of his hat. "The Raindrop Lounge is but one piece of a larger puzzle," he replied cryptically. "To unravel its secrets, you must first prove your loyalty."

He gestured to a table beside him, upon which lay a sealed envelope. "Inside this envelope is the identity of the one who betrayed you," he continued. "But you must complete a task for me before it is revealed."

Evelyn Knox, her eyes locked on the Puppetmaster, spoke with an undercurrent of defiance. "What task?"

The Puppetmaster's lips curled into a sinister smile. "There is a rival of mine, a man known as the Shadow Broker. He possesses information that I seek. Eliminate him, and the answers you seek shall be yours."

The team exchanged wary glances, the weight of the decision hanging heavily in the air. They had ventured into the Puppetmaster's lair seeking the truth, but now they were faced with a choice that would test their principles and their willingness to descend further into the abyss of darkness.

"We'll need proof of his betrayal," Mercer said, his voice a resolute command. "We won't carry out your task blindly."

The Puppetmaster nodded, as if expecting this demand. He produced a small device and handed it to Mercer. "This will record the proof you seek," he said. "But remember, time is of the essence."

With the device in hand, Mercer and his team left the room, their footsteps echoing like a solemn march in the empty warehouse. They retreated to a secluded spot outside, where they could discuss their next move in privacy.

Evelyn, her expression a mix of determination and trepidation, addressed Mercer. "Do we really have a choice, Daniel? We need that information to clear our names."

Mercer knew that the Puppetmaster's task was a dangerous one, a descent into the treacherous depths of the criminal underworld. But their pursuit of answers had brought them to this precipice, and there was no turning back.

"We'll gather the necessary information, find proof of the betrayal," Mercer said, his voice resolute. "Then, and only then, will we consider the Puppetmaster's task."

Their decision made, they set out to gather information about the Shadow Broker—a rival with a reputation for cunning and ruthlessness. The rain continued to fall, a relentless downpour that mirrored the dark path they had chosen to follow.

As they ventured further into the criminal underworld, Mercer couldn't escape the sense that they were caught in a web of deception, where loyalties shifted like the shadows and the pursuit of truth came at a staggering cost. The Puppetmaster's lair had revealed only a glimpse of the darkness that lay ahead, and the answers they sought remained elusive, concealed within a labyrinth of secrets and treachery.

Shadows of Betrayal

The rain-soaked streets of the city had taken on a ghostly pallor as Daniel Mercer and his team embarked on their perilous mission to gather evidence against the Shadow Broker—a task demanded by the enigmatic Puppetmaster in exchange for revealing the identity of their betrayer. The air was thick with tension, and the oppressive darkness seemed to seep into their very souls.

Their search for information led them through the labyrinthine alleys and dimly lit corners of the city's underworld. Mercer knew that the Shadow Broker operated in the shadows, hidden from the prying eyes of law enforcement and rival criminals alike.

Their first lead took them to a rundown bar known as "The Whispering Cane." It was a place where secrets were traded like currency, and the patrons spoke in hushed tones, mindful of the walls that had ears.

Slick Reynolds, his face hidden beneath a hood, approached the bar's owner—a portly man with a greying beard known as Big Pete. Mercer watched from a dimly lit corner as the exchange took place.

"We're looking for information on the Shadow Broker," Slick said, his voice a low murmur.

Big Pete regarded Slick with a calculating gaze before nodding slowly. "I've heard whispers," he admitted, "but I can't give you everything for free."

With a sly grin, he slid a small envelope across the bar, and Slick pocketed it discreetly. Mercer could feel the weight of their desperation growing heavier with each passing moment. They needed the information to clear their names, and the Puppetmaster's task loomed over them like a shadow.

Back in their temporary safehouse, they examined the contents of the envelope—a series of photographs and documents detailing the Shadow Broker's criminal activities. It was a damning dossier, evidence of a man who thrived in the darkness of deceit.

Maria Sanchez, her eyes scanning the documents, spoke with determination. "We have what we need. We can confront the Puppetmaster now."

But Mercer hesitated, his thoughts mired in doubt. "We still don't know the extent of the Puppetmaster's power. Confronting him without leverage could be a fatal mistake."

Evelyn Knox, her gaze steady, interjected. "We can use this information as insurance. Force the Puppetmaster to reveal the identity of our betrayer before we carry out his task."

It was a risky gambit, one that relied on the Puppetmaster's willingness to uphold his end of the bargain. But they had no other choice; their journey had brought them to this precipice, and they couldn't turn back now.

With their plan in place, Mercer and his team ventured once more into the city's criminal underworld, seeking an audience with the Puppetmaster. The rain had not abated, and the city's streets were awash with glistening reflections, a mirror to their uncertain path.

They returned to the dilapidated warehouse where they had encountered the Puppetmaster, the ominous room once again illuminated by the flickering bulb. The Puppetmaster awaited them in his ornate chair, a looming presence in the dimly lit space.

"We have what you asked for," Mercer said, his voice unwavering as he handed over the dossier of evidence against the Shadow Broker. "Now it's your turn. Reveal the identity of our betrayer."

The Puppetmaster took the dossier, his gloved fingers tracing the documents with a sense of malevolence. He seemed to relish the power he held over them, the strings he could pull in their desperate quest for answers.

"Very well," he finally said, his voice a chilling whisper. "The name you seek is Frederick Rhodes. He's a man with many faces, a chameleon who revels in deception."

Mercer's heart sank at the mention of the name. Frederick Rhodes was a name from their past—a man who had once been a trusted member of their crew. It was a betrayal that cut deep, a wound that had festered in the darkness.

Evelyn Knox, her voice tinged with anger, demanded answers. "Why did he betray us? What does he gain from it?"

The Puppetmaster leaned back in his chair, a sinister smile curling his lips. "Frederick Rhodes had debts, debts he could not repay. The Shadow Broker offered him a way out, a chance to erase his past. But in doing so, he condemned all of you."

As the Puppetmaster's words hung in the air, Mercer couldn't help but feel a sense of bitter betrayal. They had trusted Rhodes, relied on him as a member of their crew, and he had cast aside their loyalty for his own gain.

"Now that you have your answers," the Puppetmaster continued, "it is time for you to fulfill your end of the bargain. Eliminate the Shadow Broker, as we agreed."

Mercer nodded, his resolve unyielding. "We will carry out your task. But understand this, Puppetmaster—we'll be watching, and we won't forget."

Their audience with the Puppetmaster concluded, Mercer and his team left the warehouse, their footsteps echoing in the silence of the night. The revelation of their betrayer had reopened old wounds, and the path they now followed was one of vengeance and redemption.

As they ventured once more into the city's underworld, the shadows of betrayal loomed large. The Puppetmaster's task was a dangerous one, a descent into the darkest depths of the criminal underworld. But they were determined to confront the Shadow Broker, to unearth the truth that had eluded them for so long.

In a city where secrets held sway and deception reigned supreme, Mercer and his team were caught in a web of shadows, their pursuit of answers a relentless dance on the precipice of danger. The final act awaited, and the outcome remained uncertain, concealed within the cloak of night.

The Shadow Broker's Game

The city's heart pulsed with secrets and treachery as Daniel Mercer and his team embarked on their mission to confront the Shadow Broker, the man responsible for their betrayal. The relentless rain had cast a shadow over the metropolis, its glistening streets mirroring the darkness that lurked within.

The dossier they had gathered against the Shadow Broker served as both a weapon and insurance—a bargaining chip to ensure their safety during their dangerous rendezvous. The location had been arranged at a disused warehouse near the city's waterfront, a place where the criminal elite gathered to negotiate their illicit deals.

As Mercer's team approached the warehouse, they couldn't help but feel a sense of unease. The Puppetmaster's web of deceit and manipulation had brought them here, and the stakes had never been higher. They entered the abandoned building, their senses on high alert, every creak of the floorboards echoing in the eerie silence.

The interior was dimly lit by a single overhead bulb, casting long, distorted shadows on the cracked concrete floor. In the center of the room, a figure sat on a weathered leather chair, shrouded in darkness.

The Shadow Broker.

Mercer and his team approached cautiously, their eyes locked on the enigmatic figure. The man's face was concealed beneath a featureless mask, his identity a closely guarded secret.

"We have evidence against you," Mercer said, his voice unwavering. "Proof of your criminal activities."

The Shadow Broker chuckled, a sinister sound that reverberated through the room. "Ah, evidence is a fragile thing," he replied, his voice a cold, mechanical tone. "It can be manufactured, manipulated. What makes you think I'm concerned?"

Evelyn Knox, her gaze unwavering, stepped forward, holding out the dossier of evidence. "We're not here to negotiate," she said. "We're here for answers. Why did you betray us?"

The Shadow Broker's mask seemed to shift, as if he were contemplating his response. "Betrayal is a matter of perspective," he replied cryptically. "In my world, loyalty is a currency, and debts must be settled."

Mercer couldn't help but feel a sense of frustration. The Shadow Broker's words were like riddles, a maze of deception that obscured the truth.

"We need to know who you're working for," Slick Reynolds interjected, his voice taut with tension. "Who set us up at the Raindrop Lounge?"

The Shadow Broker leaned back in his chair, the mask concealing any hint of expression. "Curiosity can be a dangerous thing," he mused. "But I suppose I can indulge you. I work for a consortium—a group of powerful individuals who control the city's underworld. Their identities are a closely guarded secret."

The revelation sent shockwaves through Mercer's team. A consortium with the power to manipulate events in the criminal underworld—it was a revelation that raised more questions than answers.

"We won't be pawns in your game any longer," Mercer declared, his voice resolute. "We have leverage now, evidence that can expose you and your consortium."

The Shadow Broker's mask seemed to shift, as if he were considering his options. "Very well," he finally said. "I can offer you a deal. I will reveal the identity of your betrayer, but in exchange, you must disappear from this city forever. No more heists, no more games."

It was a tempting offer, a chance to escape the shadows that had haunted them for so long. But Mercer couldn't help but wonder if the Shadow Broker's words could be trusted.

"We need proof of the betrayal," Mercer insisted. "And we need assurance that you won't come after us."

The Shadow Broker's mask tilted slightly, as if he were contemplating his response. "Very well," he conceded. "I will provide you with proof, and you will have my word that you will no longer be pursued."

With the terms of their agreement settled, the Shadow Broker handed over a sealed envelope—a dossier that contained the damning evidence they sought. Mercer and his team left the warehouse, their footsteps heavy with the weight of their decision.

As they examined the contents of the envelope, they found photographs and documents that implicated Frederick Rhodes in their betrayal. It was irrefutable proof of their former ally's treachery, a betrayal that had torn their crew apart.

"We have what we need," Mercer said, his voice tinged with bitterness. "It's time to confront Rhodes and put an end to this."

With their evidence in hand, they tracked down Frederick Rhodes to a disused warehouse on the outskirts of the city. The rain had not abated, and the night was a canvas of shadows and secrets.

Inside the warehouse, Rhodes stood alone, his face a mask of surprise and resignation as Mercer's team confronted him with the evidence of his betrayal.

"It's over, Rhodes," Mercer said, his voice heavy with disappointment. "You betrayed us for your own gain."

Rhodes, his shoulders slumped, finally spoke. "I had debts, Daniel. I had no choice."

Evelyn Knox, her voice filled with anger, retorted, "There's always a choice, Rhodes. You chose betrayal."

As they handed Rhodes over to the authorities, Mercer couldn't help but feel a sense of closure. Their journey had been one of deception and treachery, but they had finally unraveled the truth.

With their names cleared, Mercer and his team left the city behind, disappearing into the night as they had agreed with the Shadow Broker. It was a bittersweet ending, a departure from a world of shadows and secrets.

As they ventured into the unknown, Mercer couldn't help but wonder about the consortium that controlled the city's underworld. The city was a place where power and deception intertwined, a world where loyalties were fragile and the pursuit of truth came at a staggering cost.

In the end, their journey had been a relentless dance on the precipice of danger, a descent into the shadows of betrayal. But as they left the city behind, they carried with them the knowledge that they had uncovered the truth, that they had refused to be mere pawns in a game of shadows.

The Consortium's Gambit

The city they left behind was a maze of steel and glass, its towering skyscrapers gleaming in the morning sun. As Daniel Mercer and his team drove away from the metropolis that had been their crucible of secrets and betrayal, they carried with them a bitter sense of closure and a lingering curiosity about the consortium—the powerful group that had controlled the city's criminal underworld.

Their journey had led them to the precipice of danger, and now they found themselves on a winding road, far removed from the shadowy world they had known. Mercer couldn't help but wonder about the identities of the consortium's members, the puppeteers who had orchestrated their heist and set their lives on a treacherous course.

"We need to find out more about the consortium," Mercer said, his voice tinged with determination. "We can't let them operate in the shadows any longer."

Evelyn Knox, her gaze fixed on the road ahead, nodded in agreement. "We have the evidence we need to expose them. But we'll need allies—people who can help us bring them down."

As they traveled, they reached out to their network of contacts—trusted individuals who had once operated in the criminal underworld but had since left that life behind. Each call was a risky move, a leap of faith that their allies would be willing to help.

One by one, their former associates agreed to meet them in a secluded cabin nestled deep in the woods. It was a place far removed from the city's prying eyes, a sanctuary where secrets could be exchanged without fear of retribution.

The cabin's interior was a dimly lit space, its walls adorned with hunting trophies from a bygone era. Mercer and his team gathered around a table, their allies sitting in the shadows, their faces etched with weariness and uncertainty.

"We have evidence against the consortium," Mercer began, his voice carrying the weight of their mission. "Evidence that can expose their criminal activities and bring them down."

The room fell into silence as the gravity of their words hung in the air. The former associates, some of whom had once been rivals, were now united by a common cause—the desire to dismantle the criminal empire that had held the city in its grip.

One of the allies, a woman named Isabella, spoke with a steely resolve. "We'll need a plan. Exposing the consortium won't be easy, and they won't go down without a fight."

With the allies' expertise and knowledge of the criminal underworld, they began to formulate a strategy. They would gather additional evidence, infiltrate the consortium's operations, and build a case that could withstand the scrutiny of law enforcement.

As the days turned into weeks, Mercer's team and their allies worked tirelessly, each step taking them closer to their goal. They uncovered the consortium's illicit dealings, its connections to corrupt officials, and the extent of its power and influence.

But as they delved deeper into the web of deception, they realized the consortium's reach extended far beyond what they had initially imagined. Its members were hidden among the city's elite, their wealth and influence shielded by layers of secrecy.

"We need a way to expose them without risking our lives," Slick Reynolds said, his face etched with concern. "They have resources we can't match."

Evelyn Knox, her eyes filled with determination, had an idea. "We'll need to leverage public opinion. Expose the consortium's criminal activities to the world, and they won't be able to hide any longer."

Their plan was audacious—a massive data leak that would reveal the consortium's darkest secrets to the media and law enforcement. They would need a whistleblower, someone from within the consortium who was willing to expose the truth.

With their allies' help, they reached out to potential whistleblowers, individuals who had grown disillusioned with the consortium's actions and were willing to risk everything for justice.

Finally, they found a whistleblower—a high-ranking member of the consortium who had become disenchanted with the criminal empire's ruthlessness. The whistleblower, a man named Gregory Tremaine, agreed to provide them with the evidence they needed to expose the consortium's crimes.

The day of the data leak arrived, a day when secrets would be laid bare for the world to see. Mercer's team and their allies gathered in a makeshift command center, their fingers poised over keyboards and their hearts pounding with anticipation.

As the evidence of the consortium's criminal activities was released to the media, shockwaves rippled through the city. Scandals and revelations were front-page news, and the consortium's members found themselves exposed to the harsh light of public scrutiny.

The city's law enforcement agencies launched investigations, and arrests were made. The consortium's power crumbled, its members scrambling to protect themselves from the fallout.

In the midst of the chaos, Mercer and his team stood on the precipice of victory, their mission to expose the consortium's criminal empire a success. But the cost had been high, and the shadows of their past still lingered.

As they watched the city's underworld crumble, Mercer couldn't help but wonder if they had finally escaped the darkness that had haunted them for so long. The pursuit of truth had been a relentless journey, a descent into the abyss of danger and betrayal. But in the end, they had refused to be mere pawns in a game of shadows, and justice had prevailed.

www.ingramcontent.com/pod-product-compliance
Lightning Source LLC
LaVergne TN
LVHW061604070526
838199LV00077B/7166